Contents

Published by The Royal Society for the Protection of Birds, The Lodge, Sandy, Bedfordshire SG19 2DL.

Great care has been taken throughout this book to ensure accuracy, but the RSPB cannot accept any responsibility for any error that may occur.

Cover photograph: Kingfisher by Jan Haladay (RSPB Images).
Insets by C H Gomersall (RSPB Images).
Opposite photograph: Strumpshaw Fen by M W Richards (RSPB Images).

Maps: Drawing Attention. Illustrations: John Busby and Dan Powell

ISBN 0 903138 96 4
Registered charity number 207076
49/681/97-98

Introduction

Mike Read

Titchwell Marsh Nature Reserve

RSPB nature reserves provide an excellent opportunity to watch birds and other wildlife in some of the most beautiful parts of the country. There are over 140 RSPB nature reserves throughout the United Kingdom, covering more than 240,000 acres (97,000 hectares). Creating nature reserves is one of the most effective ways of conserving wild birds and the places where they live. The RSPB has been managing nature reserves for over 60 years and our knowledge is renowned.

RSPB nature reserves serve two purposes; the conservation of wild birds and their habitats and developing the public's interest and concern for birds and wildlife.

Saving a place for birds

The birds and wildlife on our reserves must always come first. To achieve the correct balance between wildlife and people, on a few reserves where the habitat and wildlife are especially fragile, we have to restrict visitor access.

This guide aims to help you enjoy the birds and wildlife on our nature reserves. We hope that you will enjoy using it and, more importantly, enjoy visiting many of our nature reserves.

The RSPB . . .

- is Europe's largest wildlife conservation charity and the UK partner of BirdLife International;

- is supported by 967,000 members;

- has 175 members' groups, which raise funds and public awareness of our activities;

- benefits from 20,000 days of voluntary work each year;

- leads in bird conservation research, both in the UK and abroad;

- is involved in conservation projects in over 20 countries worldwide;

- provides advice and training for teachers from junior school to further and higher education establishments.

Visiting RSPB nature reserves

Visitors are welcome at the nature reserves in this guide. For each reserve we list the facilities available. At some, such as Pulborough Brooks and Vane Farm, we offer tearooms, car parks and shops. However, we do not provide a full-range of facilities on all of our nature reserves. This is either because the habitat is not suitable for large numbers of visitors or because of financial restraints. On all our nature reserves, the interests of wildlife must come first.

When can I visit?
The opening times are given for each reserve. Opening times for visitor and information centres, hides, car parks and toilets on some nature reserves may not coincide with reserve opening hours.

Can I go where I like on a reserve?
On many reserves only certain areas will be open to the public, the remainder being kept quiet for wildlife. To avoid unnecessary disturbance, please keep to the marked trails and paths.

Are dogs welcome on RSPB nature reserves?
Unfortunately, no (registered guide dogs excepted). This is to prevent unnecessary disturbance to wildlife.

Can I visit by public transport?
Yes! For those who want to use public transport to visit our nature reserves, the nearest railway station is given. In most cases, a bus or taxi will be needed to complete the journey to the reserve.

What should I wear?
Even in the summer be prepared for a sudden change in the weather, particularly on exposed and upland reserves. Carry warm and waterproof clothes just in case. On some reserves the paths may be uneven and rugged so stout footwear should be worn. Wellington boots are recommended for some wetland reserves.

Are children welcome on RSPB nature reserves?
Yes! All members of the family can find something of interest on our reserves. Those with visitor centres are particularly suitable for families. Some paths on some reserves may be unsuitable for pushchairs and young children may need to be carried.

Will there be someone to answer my questions?
Where possible on our most visited reserves a member of staff or volunteer will be pleased to answer any queries you may have. However, on some of our less visited reserves a member of staff or

C H Gomersall (RSPB Images)

RSPB nature reserves are wonderful places to enjoy the countryside.

volunteer may not be available. Many reserves have some form of information centre. These range from purpose-built visitor centres with teaching facilities, shops and toilets to more low-key outdoor interpretative displays. The centres' opening hours may differ from those of the reserves.

How do I explore the reserve?
On most nature reserves there are specially laid out nature trails and way-marked paths. Some reserves have trail leaflets, while on others there may be path-side display boards. To avoid disturbing wildlife we ask you to keep to the paths.

Can I get something to eat and drink?
Where appropriate we are introducing refreshment facilities on nature reserves. Some, such as Pulborough Brooks and Leighton Moss, have a tearoom where you can get a light meal or snack; others, such as Lochwinnoch and Ynys-hir, have more limited facilities, such as vending machines. On some reserves it is not possible to provide refreshments, but picnic tables are often available.

Is there anything else to see on an RSPB nature reserve?
Yes. Lots of other wildlife, from mammals to insects, from fungi to flowers can be found on our nature reserves. For each reserve, we give a brief description of what other wildlife you might see.

Many of our nature reserves have programmes of events throughout the year, including guided walks, bat evenings, dawn chorus walks and talks. For more information on these events, contact the reserve direct.

Can I help on an RSPB nature reserve?
We always welcome volunteers to work on our nature reserves. You may want to do practical management work or be happier helping in one of the shops. If you would like further information on how you can help, please contact our Reserves Management Department at The Lodge. If you do not want to work on a reserve, but would like to help us, there are many other things you can do, from helping at one of our offices to joining one of our 175 local members' groups. For more information please contact the Youth and Volunteer Department at The Lodge.

Are school children welcome?
Yes. The RSPB offers a comprehensive service for schools on many nature reserves. The education programmes are designed to complement the relevant national curricula. The programmes are run by trained RSPB teacher naturalists and the emphasis is on a hands-on approach to environmental education. For further details please contact the Education Department at The Lodge.

C H Gomersall (RSPB Images)

Young people are welcome on RSPB nature reserves.

What birds can I expect to see?
For each reserve we give you an idea of the birds you might expect to see and the time of year that they are there. Because of their very nature, we cannot guarantee that you will see any or all of the birds listed.

How to use this guide

The reserves are listed alphabetically by country. Written directions to nature reserves are given.

P   Car park

🚲   Bicycle rack

🏬   On some reserves there is an admission charge for non-members of the RSPB and YOC. This charge is refunded if you join the Society on the day of your visit. Family tickets for two adults and up to four children are available on many charging reserves. The prices quoted are correct at time of going to press, but are subject to change.

🚻   Toilets are available on or beside the reserve. Where possible on our major reserves we do try to provide toilet facilities. However, it is not always possible to do so.

♿   Toilets suitable for visitors with disabilities.

👶   Baby changing facilities

🍽   Tearoom with a full range of hot and cold drinks, snacks and light meals.

☕   Drinks and light snacks available

🍴   Picnic area

S   Main shop
A number of reserves have RSPB shops selling an extensive range of goods from binoculars and books to bird food and feeders.

s   Small retail outlet

🔭   Binocular hire

AV   Closed circuit TV

🚶   Group bookings. Where possible a member of staff will be happy to escort groups around the reserve. Any group of over 15 should contact the warden to make suitable arrangements.

🚶   Guided walks and special events.

♿   There are facilities suitable for visitors with special needs on many of our nature reserves. Access is being constantly upgraded. In many instances, hides have been adapted for wheelchair access and special paths and boardwalks have been installed. A free leaflet with more details is available from RSPB headquarters at The Lodge.

T   Environmental education programmes available, enquire at the reserve for details.

F-H

Country

P # Reserve name, county
🏬
🍴
🚶   A brief description of the reserve and the wildlife that is found there

🚶   **Opening times:** opening times and
♿   access restrictions
T   🏬 entrance charge
Location: directions to the reserve
Map page where map can be found.
⇄ Nearest railway station;
🚌 Bus route.
☎ Reserve telephone number
i nearest tourist information office telephone number
Nature trail Number of trails and distances
Visitor centre or **Information centre**
Birdwatching hides number of hides and access
Additional information

England

The RSPB is committed to
minimising the environmental
impact of transport. When
visiting our nature reserves,
please consider using public
transpot or a bicycle.
If you do use a car, please
consider sharing the
journey with others.

Map

Map labels:

Blackpool, Preston, M55, MARSHSIDE, Southport, Blackburn, M65, DEE ESTUARY, Bolton, M6, M66, Liverpool, M58, Wigan, Manchest, M62, Birkenhead, Stockp, M53, M56, Chester, A54, A41, A534, M6, Wrexham, A525, A53, A49, A41, A5, A442, A4442, Wolverhampton, A456, Worcester, A44, A4103, M50, Ross-on-Wye, Cheltenha, HIGHNAM WOODS, A40, Gloucest, SYMONDS YAT, B423, M5, NAGSHEAD, A433, Chippenham, Bristol, Bath, A36, WEST SEDGEMOOR, A361, CHAPEL WOOD, A367, Minehead, Glastonbury, A39, Warminster, Barnstaple, A399, A396, A368, A39, A37, GARSTO WOOD, Taunton, A372, A303, A361, A386, A377, A378, Yeovil, A39, A396, M5, A303, Ilminster, Blandford Forum, Okehampton, A30, A358, A37, Launceston, A3052, A35, Dorchester, Po, Exeter, A379, A352, Newquay, A39, A38, A388, A386, A38, Weymouth, ARNE, HAYLE ESTUARY, Paignton, AYLESBEARE COMMON, LODMOO, A30, Redruth, A390, Plymouth, EXE ESTUARY, RADIPOLE LAKE, Penzance, A394, Helston, MARAZION MARSH

6

FAIRBURN INGS
Leeds
Selby
Kingston-upon-Hull
Pontefract
Scunthorpe
Rotherham
BLACKTOFT SANDS

Mansfield
Lincoln
COOMBES VALLEY
CHURNET VALLEY
SNETTISHAM
Derby
Nottingham
Uttoxeter

SURLINGHAM CHURCH MARSH

TITCHWELL MARSH
Wells-next-the-Sea
STRUMPSHAW FEN
BERNEY MARSHES
Hunstanton
King's Lynn
BREYDON WATER
LITTLE TERN WATCHING
Great Yarmouth

SANDWELL VALLEY
Norwich
Lowestoft
Nuneaton
Birmingham
Coventry
OUSE WASHES
Kettering
Ely
Thetford
Southwold
Northampton
Warwick
THE LODGE
Cambridge
Saxmundham
MINSMERE
NORTH WARREN
Aldeburgh
Bedford
Sandy
WOLVES WOOD
Ipswich
FOWLMERE
Hadleigh
HAVERGATE ISLAND
Stevenage
RYE HOUSE MARSH
Felixstowe
Harwich
Oxford
Luton
Hertford
Harlow
Colchester
STOUR ESTUARY
CHURCH WOOD
Southend-on-Sea
High Wycombe
NORTHWARD HILL
Reading
Grain
NOR MARSH & MOTNEY HILL
Slough
Sheerness
ELMLEY MARSHES
Newbury
Ramsgate
BLEAN WOODS
Maidstone
Canterbury
Basingstoke
Andover
Farnham
Guildford
Sevenoaks
Tonbridge
Ashford
Dover
Crawley
East Grinstead
Folkestone
Salisbury
Winchester
Horsham
Billingshurst
TUDELEY WOODS
Royal Tunbridge Wells
New Romney
Southampton
Lewes
Lydd
DUNGENESS
Bournemouth
Bognor Regis
Brighton
Newhaven
Eastbourne
Hastings
FORE WOOD
Portsmouth
LANGSTONE HARBOUR
PULBOROUGH BROOKS

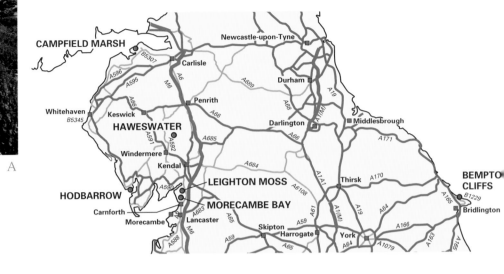

A

P Arne, Dorset

To visit Arne is to glimpse the Dorset of
Thomas Hardy. Special heathland
wildlife survives here, including
Dartford warblers and nightjars, all six
species of British reptiles and 22 species
of dragonflies. The reserve overlooks
Poole Harbour, where in winter you can
watch large numbers of waders and
wildfowl, including black-tailed godwits,
brent geese and red-breasted mergansers.
Opening times: only the Shipstal part of
the reserve is open to visitors (at all
times).
non-members – £1 car parking fee.
Location: east of Wareham off A351 to
Swanage, taking turning signposted to
Arne, or take road from Stoborough
village. **Map** pages 6-7.
Wareham (4 miles / 6.5 km);
stop in Stoborough (3 miles / 5 km),
Poole to Swanage service, hourly.
☎ 01929 553360
i 01929 422885
Nature trail (1 mile / 1.6 km) and path to
the beach
Birdwatching hides 1, a mile from car
park, unsuitable for wheelchairs.

P Aylesbeare Common,
Devon

This quiet area of Devon heathland is
important for Dartford warblers,
nightjars and stonechats. Its sheltered
wooded fringes, streams and ponds
abound with butterflies, dragonflies
and damselflies.
Opening times: open at all times.
Location: 5 miles / 8 km east of J30 of
the M5 at Exeter, 0.5 mile / 0.8 km past
the Halfway Inn on the B3052, turn
right, signposted Hawkerland.
Map page 6.
Exeter Central or St Davids
(10 miles / 16 km);
half-hourly 52 and 52A Exeter to
Sidmouth service stops past car park.
☎ 01395 567880
i 01404 813964
Nature trail (2 miles / 3 km), with many
paths (1 farm track which crosses the
heath is suitable for wheelchairs and
pushchairs).

Bempton Cliffs, East Yorkshire

P
🚲
🚏
🏪
🚻♿
☕
S
⚑
♿
T

With over three miles of sheer cliffs, rising to 400 feet/120 m, Bempton is the best place in England to see breeding seabirds (over 200,000). Five safe viewing points give spectacular close-up views of puffins, gannets, guillemots, razorbills, kittiwakes and fulmars between April and mid-August. At other times there are migrating birds to be seen and possibly seals and porpoises. The shop has an extensive range of RSPB goods and books.

Opening times: reserve – open at all times; visitor centre – March to November 10 am to 5 pm, winter weekends only 9.30 am to 4 pm.
🏪 non-members – £1.50 car parking fee.
Location: On cliff road from village of Bempton which is on B1229 road from Flamborough to Filey. **Map** page 8.
🚆 Bempton 1.5 miles/2.5 km;
🚌 Bridlington to Bempton 1.5 miles/2.5 km.
☎ 01262 851179
i 01262 673474
Visitor centre
There are cliff-top walks up to 1 mile/1.6 km (the first two viewpoints at 200 yards/183 m and 400 yards/365 m are suitable for wheelchairs and pushchairs).

B

M W Richards (RSPB Images)

C H Gomersall (RSPB Images)

Gannet

Bempton Cliffs, home to thousands of nesting seabirds.

P Ⓐ Ⓧ Berney Marshes and Breydon Water, Norfolk

Experience the wide open spaces of grazing marshes and mudflats at Berney Marshes and Breydon Water. There is a short nature trail and a viewing screen overlooking the marshes. Details of boat trips are available from the warden.

Opening times: open at all times.

Location: park at the Asda car park near Great Yarmouth railway station (walk to Berney Marshes 8 mile/13 km round trip). Boat trips are available from Goodchild Marina, Burgh Castle.

Map page 7.

⇌ Great Yarmouth for Breydon Water and Berney Arms halt for Berney Marshes;

🚌 Norwich to Great Yarmouth.

☎ 01493 700645

i 01493 842195

Nature trail (0.5 mile/0.8 km).

P Blacktoft Sands, Yorkshire

With its 474 acres/192 ha of tidal reedbeds, saltmarsh, mudflats and brackish lagoons, Blacktoft Sands has a wide variety of special birds, including bearded tits, marsh harriers and avocets. In spring and autumn, many more birds call in on migration.

Bearded tit

C H Gomersall (RSPB Images)

Blacktoft Sands

Opening times: open daily 9 am to 5 pm (closed 25 December)
🎫 non-members – adult £2.50, child 50p, concession £1.50, family ticket £4.50.
Location: On the A161 east of Goole through Reedness and Ousefleet.
Map page 7.
🚌 bus stop opposite reserve entrance. Buses from Goole 2–3 hourly, Monday to Saturday.
☎ 01405 704665
i 01482 593959
Nature trail (0.5 mile/0.8 km, 0.25 mile/0.4 km of which suitable for wheelchairs and pushchairs)
Birdwatching hides 6 (5 wheelchair accessible). Information hide.

S Knell (RSPB Images)

Little ringed plover

P Blean Woods, Kent

Blean Woods is one of the largest areas of ancient broadleaved woodland in southern Britain. Woodpeckers are plentiful, while in the summer there are about 30 pairs of nightingales and a few redstarts. The reserve is one of the few places in Britain where you can find the heath fritillary butterfly.
Opening times: the paths are open at all times. The car park is open from 8 am to 9 pm.
Location: signposted from Rough Common, which is north-west of

Canterbury off the A2 to Dover or A290 to Whitstable. **Map** page 7.
🚆 Canterbury East (2 miles/3 km), Canterbury West (1.75 mile/3 km);
🚌 Canterbury to Rough Common stops outside reserve entrance.
☎ 01227 462491
i 01227 766567
Nature trails 4 (ranging from 1 to 7 miles/1.6 to 11 km), mostly suitable for pushchairs, but all trails may be muddy at times. The green trail is suitable for wheelchair users. The stone track along the reserve boundary is flat and can be used at all times.

B-C

P Campfield Marsh, Cumbria

Campfield Marsh, on the Solway estuary, has saltmarsh, wet grassland and areas of open water. At high tide, thousands of wading birds including oystercatchers, knots, grey plovers and bar-tailed godwits roost. In the winter, wildfowl use the grassland and open water areas. The wader roost can be seen from the lay-bys along the road edging the estuary and saltmarsh.
Opening times: open at all times.
Location: 3 miles/5 km west of Bowness-on-Solway.
Map page 8.
🚌 there are infrequent services to Bowness-on-Solway from Carlisle.
☎ 016973 51330
i 01228 512444

Grey plover

11

Chapel Wood, Devon

This small but varied, mainly deciduous, woodland has a good range of woodland birds, including breeding pied flycatchers. The remains of an old hill fort and a historic chapel with a well are also interesting.

Opening times: open at all times.

Location: 1.5 miles/2.5 km west of A361 (2 miles/3 km north of Braunton). Signposted from Spreacombe. **Map** page 6.

≈ Barnstaple 8 miles/13 km;
🚌 stop 1.5 miles/2.5 km (Headon Mills stop) Barnstaple, Braunton and Ilfracombe service.

☎ 01271 870713
𝑖 01271 388583

Nature trails (up to 1.5 miles/2.5 km).
Lay-by parking

Church Wood, Buckinghamshire

This small reserve forms part of the extensive Chiltern woodlands and is a mixture of beech, ash and oak. Some parts of it are hazel coppice. Woodpeckers, nuthatches and blackcaps are among the birds breeding in the wood. In the spring the woodland floor is covered with flowering bluebells.

Opening times: open at all times.

Location: About 3 miles/5 km from J2 M40 in Hedgerley village. Take the small private track beside village pond next to pub. Park off the track or in the village. **Map** page 7.

≈ Gurrards Cross 8 miles/13 km;
🚌 Slough to Hedgerley.

☎ 01295 253330
𝑖 01628 781110

Nature trail 2 marked paths (shortest 0.5 mile/0.8 km, longest 1.25 miles/2 km).

R Revels (RSPB Images)

High brown fritillary butterflies can be found at Coombes Valley.

Coombes Valley, Staffordshire

A walk through this beautiful steep-sided, wooded valley in summer could reveal special birds such as pied flycatchers, redstarts and wood warblers, or a dipper. It is an excellent place for butterflies – including the rare high brown fritillary. From the two birdwatching hides you can watch very different aspects of the reserve – the tree canopy and a small pool.

Opening times: reserve – daily (closed 25, 26 December) 9 am to 9 pm or dusk (last entry 2 hours before closing); visitor centre – weekends and weekdays during busy periods.

Location: off the A523 road to Ashbourne, 3 miles/5 km south-east of Leek. Take minor road to Apesford (as signposted) for 1 mile/1.6 km. **Map** page 7.

≈ Stoke-on-Trent 13 miles/21 km.

☎ 01538 384017
𝑖 01538 381000

Information centre

P Dungeness, Kent

Situated on a unique shingle bank protruding into the English Channel, Dungeness has one of South-East England's most important breeding colonies of gulls and terns.

The RSPB manages the pits and pools for the large numbers of wildfowl, including Bewick's swans, gadwalls and smews, that are present in the winter. Wading birds visit the reserve on their spring and autumn migrations. The reserve is also excellent for seeing other migrating birds.

You can birdwatch from the visitor centre with its large picture windows, or go to one of the six birdwatching hides around the reserve. The centre sells a wide range of RSPB goods and wildlife books and has interpretative displays about this special reserve and its wildlife.
Opening times: reserve – daily (closed Tuesdays) 9 am to sunset; visitor centre – 9 am to 5 pm (9 am to 4 pm November to February).

non-members – adult £2, child 50p, concession £1.50, family ticket £4.
Location: signposted off the Lydd to Dungeness road 10 miles / 16 km east of Rye. **Map** page 7.
Rye (10 miles / 16 km).
☎ 01797 320588
i 01797 364044
Visitor centre
Nature trail (about 1 mile / 1.6 km) wheelchair and pushchair accessible
Birdwatching hides 6 (most wheelchair accessible).

D

Smews are regular winter visitors to Dungeness.

S Knell (RSPB Images)

Dungeness Nature Reserve

R Horne (RSPB Images)

E-F

P Elmley Marshes, Kent

The wet grassland of Elmley Marshes attracts thousands of ducks, geese and wading birds in the winter. Hen harriers, merlins, peregrines and short-eared owls can also be seen during the winter. In the summer, many wading birds, including the elegant avocet, breed on the reserve.
Opening times: open daily (closed Tuesdays) 9 am to 9 pm or sunset when earlier.
non-members – adult £2.50, child 50p, concession £1.50, family £4.50.
Location: signposted off the A249 to Sheerness on the Isle of Sheppey, 1 mile/1.6 km beyond the Kingsferry Bridge. **Map** page 7.
Swaleholt (request stop) 3 miles/5 km; nearest stop at Queenborough (4 miles/6.5 km).
☎ 01795 665969 or 01273 775333
i 01795 534542
Birdwatching hides 5 – there is a 1.25 mile/2 km walk to the nearest hide and 6 mile/9.5 km round trip to the furthest hide (special access arrangements can be made for disabled and elderly visitors).

Short-eared owl

R Glover (RSPB Images)

P Exe Estuary, Devon

This reserve covers two separate areas of coastal grazing marsh on opposite sides of the estuary – Exminster Marshes and Bowling Green Marsh. In spring you can watch breeding lapwings and redshanks and in winter during floods and at high tide there are thousands of roosting and feeding curlews, lapwings and wigeons.
Opening times: access at all times but restricted to public footpaths and hide at Bowling Green Marsh.
Location: Exminster Marshes, east of Exminster village, 5 miles/8 km south of Exeter; Bowling Green Marsh, on the outskirts of Topsham, 5 miles/8 km south-east of Exeter, signposted from Holman Way car park, Topsham.
Map page 6.
Exminster Marshes ⇌ Exeter station 5 miles/8 km, Exeter to Dawlish service stops at roundabout on A379 (Swan's Nest) every 20 minutes most of day.
Bowling Green Marsh ⇌ Topsham station 5 minutes' walk, Exeter to Topsham service stops at Quay every 15 minutes most of day. A foot ferry is sometimes available between the two parts of the reserve.
☎ 01392 833632 *i* 01392 265700
Birdwatching hides 1 and roadside viewing at Bowling Green Marsh suitable for wheelchair users (10–15 minutes from car park).

P Fairburn Ings, West Yorkshire

Easily accessible just off the A1, Fairburn is an ideal place to see wetland birds at close quarters throughout the year. In winter the large numbers of wildfowl include over 50 whooper swans. In summer breeding waders include redshanks, snipe and lapwings. Many waders visit on migration each year and in spring black terns usually appear among the terns on passage.

C H Gomersall (RSPB Images)

F

Fairburn Ings

Opening times: main car park – daily 9 am to dusk; 2 public paths – open at all times; visitor centre – weekends and bank holidays 10 am to 5 pm.
Location: 4 miles/6.5 km north of M62, immediately to west of A1; 5 miles/8 km north-east of Castleford, signposted from Allerton Bywater off A656. **Map** page 7.
⇴ Castleford 5 miles/8 km;
🚌 to Allerton Bywater (1.5 miles/2.5 km from visitor centre), frequent from Castleford and Leeds. Very infrequent service to Fairburn and Newton from Castleford, Pontefract and Selby.
☎ 01977 673257
i 01924 305000
Visitor centre (wheelchair accessible)
Nature trails 2 (1 pushchair accessible), boardwalk (wheelchair/pushchair accessible), views from causeway.
Birdwatching hides 6 (1 wheelchair accessible).

M Hamblin (RSPB Images)

Whooper swans are regular winter visitors at Fairburn Ings

P Fore Wood, East Sussex

This small woodland reserve is managed by coppicing. A wide range of woodland birds breed including nightingales, spotted flycatchers and great and lesser spotted woodpeckers. Bluebells, wood anemones and early purple orchids are abundant in the spring. As the nature trail in the wood can be muddy, stout footwear is recommended.
Opening times: open at all times.
Location: on the edge of Crowhurst, 2 miles/3 km south-west of Telham on the A2100. **Map** page 7.
⇴ Crowhurst 0.25 mile/400 m.
☎ 01273 775333
i 01424 773727
Parking: please park at Crowhurst village hall and walk the short distance to the reserve entrance.
Nature trail 1

Redshank

P Fowlmere, Cambridgeshire

Fowlmere's reedbeds and pools are fed by natural chalk springs; a crystal clear chalk stream runs through the reserve. Special birds include kingfishers and water rails throughout the year, breeding sedge and reed warblers and a roost of reed buntings in the winter.

Opening times: open at all times.
non-members – £1 donation.
Location: 7 miles/11 km south of Cambridge between Fowlmere and Melbourn. **Map** page 7.
Shepreth (2 miles/3 km).
01763 208978
i 01223 322640
Nature trail (1 mile/1.6 km) part wheelchair/pushchair accessible
Birdwatching hides 4

P Garston Wood, Dorset

This ancient coppiced wood is especially worth visiting in spring, when it has breathtaking carpets of bluebells, wood anemones and primroses. Listen too for the song of the nightingale and turtle dove and look out for signs of badgers and fallow deer.

Opening times: open at all times.
Location: on the road to Broad Chalke, 1 mile/1.6 km north of Sixpenny Handley which is reached from the main Salisbury to Blandford road (A354). **Map** page 6.
Salisbury (13 miles/21 km).
01392 432691 or 01929 553360
i 01258 454770

P Gayton Sands – Dee Estuary, Cheshire

High tide is the time to birdwatch at Gayton Sands. From the Old Baths car park near The Boathouse public house at Parkgate, you can watch large flocks of wading birds driven up onto the saltmarsh. In autumn and winter there

are outstanding flocks of pintails, teals, wigeons and shelducks. Please do not walk on the saltmarsh: the tides are dangerous.

Opening times: open at all times.
Location: Parkgate is reached from the A540 Chester to Hoylake road, via the B5135. **Map** page 6.
Neston 2 miles/3 km;
Parkgate every hour.
0151 336 7681
i 01244 317962

Great Yarmouth, Norfolk

Each year, the UK's largest colony of little terns breeds on the North Denes beach at Great Yarmouth. To protect these vulnerable birds the RSPB operates a special wardening scheme. Visitors can watch the birds between mid-May and the end of July.

P Havergate Island, Suffolk

This small island in the River Ore is an important breeding place for avocets, Sandwich and common terns. Access to the island is by boat only.

Opening times: access via boat. April to August – first and third weekends of the month and every Thursday; September to March – first Saturday of the month.
RSPB and YOC members – £3; non-members – £5.
Location: for boat trips meet at Orford Quay. **Map** page 7.
Woodbridge (10 miles/16 km);
infrequent service to Orford.
Reserve address: if you would like to visit please write to the warden for more information. RSPB Havergate Island Nature Reserve, 30 Munday's Lane, Orford, Woodbridge, Suffolk IP12 2LX.
01394 450732 *i* 01728 453637
Nature trail (1.5 miles/2.5 km)
Birdwatching hides 8

P Haweswater, Cumbria

Haweswater is the only place in England where golden eagles nest. An observation point is open during the breeding season. It is reached from the western end of Haweswater, 1.25 miles (2 km) along an uneven path.
Opening times: the reserve is always open; observation point 8 am to 6 pm April to August.
Location: from the M6 (J39 or J40) follow roads to Brampton and then Haweswater or Mardale. **Map** page 8.
≈ Penrith (10 miles/16 km)
☎ 01931 713376
i 01768 867466

P Hayle Estuary, Cornwall

This most south-westerly estuary in the United Kingdom is a good place to watch birds in autumn and winter. Because it never freezes, it is important for migrating and wintering wildfowl (wigeon, teal and shelduck) and waders (dunlin, curlew and grey plover).
Opening times: open at all times.
Location: in town of Hayle, 5 miles/8 km north-east of Penzance. **Map** page 6.
≈ Hayle, Lelant Saltings and Lelant;
🚌 St Ives to Hayle service, Penzance to Truro service.
☎ 01736 810783 (9 am – 5 pm)
i 01736 62207
Parking (outside opening hours only) and birdwatching hide in grounds of Quay House Inn.

P ♿ Highnam Woods, Gloucestershire

With its carpets of bluebells and primroses, this is an ideal reserve to visit in the spring when the nightingales can be heard. A winter feeding-station at the hide attracts many birds such as tits, finches and woodpeckers.

Opening times: open at all times.
Location: 3 miles/5 km west of Gloucester on the A40 Gloucester to Ross-on-Wye road. **Map** page 6.
≈ Gloucester (3 miles/5 km);
🚌 Gloucester to Cinderford.
☎ 01594 562852
i 01452 421188
Nature trail can be muddy (1.5 miles/2.5 km)
Birdwatching hides 1 (wheelchair accessible).

P Hodbarrow, Cumbria

Large numbers of wading birds and waterfowl can be seen on the freshwater lagoons. In the summer three species of terns nest on the reserve and can be seen well from the hide on the sea-wall.
Opening times: open at all times.
Location: 2 miles/3 km from Millom. **Map** page 8.
≈ and 🚌 Millom (2 miles/3 km).
☎ 016973 51330
i 01229 587120
Birdwatching hide 1 (wheelchair accessible).

Langstone Harbour, Hampshire

The reserve is made up of mudflats, creeks with saltmarsh and shingle islands in Langstone Harbour. Little terns, ringed plovers and redshanks breed here. In the winter, over 7,000 brent geese spend the winter here, along with teals, shelducks, dunlins and oystercatchers. While there is no access, good views of the reserve can be obtained from a number of viewpoints and car parks on the surrounding roads.
Opening times: open at all times.
Location: Off the A27/A3 roundabout south-west of Havant.
Map page 7.
≈ Bedhampton 1 mile/1.6 km
☎ 01273 775333
i 01705 826722

L

Mark Hamblin (RSPB Images)

Leighton Moss Nature Reserve in spring.

Leighton Moss, Lancashire

The largest remaining reedbed in north-west England, with shallow meres and fringing sedge and woodland, attract a wonderful range of wildlife to Leighton Moss. Among its special birds are breeding bitterns, bearded tits and marsh harriers, with water rails and pochards, and its mammals include otters as well as roe and red deer.

You can take your pick of long or short nature trails – shorter ones are suitable for wheelchairs and pushchairs.

Of the five birdwatching hides, four have wheelchair access. Children as well as adults will enjoy finding out more about the reserve from the imaginative displays in the visitor centre.

Opening times: reserve – daily (closed 25 December) 9 am to 9 pm or dusk; visitor centre – daily 10 am to 5 pm.

non-members – adult £3.50, child £1, concession £2, family ticket £7.

Location: 2 miles / 3 km north of Carnforth, Leighton Moss is signposted from the A6 north of Junction 35a of the M6. **Map** page 8.

Silverdale 200 yards / 183 m;
approximately every 2 hours.
☎ 01524 701601
i 01524 582808
Visitor centre
Nature trails
Birdwatching hides 5 (4 wheelchair accessible).

Marsh harrier

Bittern

The Lodge, Bedfordshire

P
🚲
🏠
♟♦♿ᵂᶜ
☕
🪑
S
🍴
👫
🏃
♿

This reserve is a mixture of woodland, heathland and includes the formal gardens of the RSPB's UK headquarters. You can watch many birds feeding on the birdtables from the Lake Hide in winter. The formal gardens are peat free and run by organic methods. The RSPB shop stocks a wide range of gifts, books and souvenirs.
Opening times: reserve – daily 9 am to 9 pm (or sunset when earlier); shop – 9 am to 5 pm weekdays, 10 am to 5 pm weekends.
🏠 non-members – adult £2, child 50p, concession £1, family ticket £4.
Location: 1 mile/1.6 km east of Sandy on the B1042 to Potton. **Map** page 7.
🚉 Sandy (1 mile/1.6 km); 🚌 frequent services from Bedford to Sandy; infrequent services pass reserve.
☎ 01767 680541
i 01767 682728

Nature trail – Up to 3.5 miles/5.5 km, 1 path and gardens wheelchair/pushchair accessible
Birdwatching hide 1, wheelchair accessible – parking 50 yards/45 m.

G. Moffatt (RSPB Images)

Great spotted woodpecker

C H Gomersall (RSPB Images)

The Lodge, UK headquarters of the RSPB.

L

Lodmoor, Dorset

This reserve always has something of interest. There is a grazing marsh with dykes, shallow pools, reedbed and scrub. Bearded tits and Cetti's warblers are around all year and autumn migration can be spectacular, with hundreds of swallows, martins and yellow wagtails, as well as a range of waders.

Opening times: open at all times.
Location: to the north-east of Weymouth, 1 mile / 1.6 km from the town centre, along A353 road to Wareham. **Map** page 6.
≠ Weymouth (1 mile / 1.6 km);
🚌 frequent local service Overcombe Corner, Lodmoor Country Park.
☎ 01305 778313
i 01305 785747
Nature trail – Circular (2 miles / 3 km)
Birdwatching hides 3, 2 are 100 yards / 90 m from the Preston Beach car park.

Marazion Marsh, Cornwall

Overlooking St Michael's Mount, this reserve has Cornwall's largest reedbed with breeding reed, sedge and Cetti's warblers, and a huge variety of plants and insects. In August and September two special birds visit on migration – spotted crake and aquatic warbler.

Opening times: open at all times.
Location: at Mount's Bay, opposite St Michael's Mount, 2 miles / 3 km east of Penzance. **Map** page 6.
≠ Penzance (2 miles / 3 km); 🚌 daily from Penzance, stopping at Marazion 0.25 mile / 0.4 km from reserve.

☎ 01736 810783 (9 am to 5 pm)
i 01736 62207
Birdwatching hides 1
Guided walks and special events May–September.

Marshside, Merseyside

Part of the internationally important Ribble Estuary, Marshside has some of the best lowland wet grassland in the north-west of England. It is an important refuge in winter for pink-footed geese, wigeons, black-tailed godwits and golden plovers and in spring provides nesting places for lapwings and redshanks, which are declining elsewhere.

Opening times: Roads alongside fields open at all times.
Location: 2 miles / 3 km north of Southport town centre on the coastal road (Marine Drive). **Map** page 6.
≠ Southport Chapel Street;
🚌 Marshside Road stop 100 yards / 90 m from reserve, routes 4, 4A and 104.
☎ 01704 880797 (9 am to 5 pm)
i 01704 533333
Toilets – Churchtown Health Centre
Toilets for the disabled – Southport Pier.

L-M

G Downey (RSPB Images)

Black-tailed godwits

Avocet

Minsmere, Suffolk

P

Set on the beautiful Suffolk coast, Minsmere offers both families and birdwatchers alike an enjoyable day out. Nature trails take you through a variety of habitats to the excellent birdwatching hides (many of which are accessible to wheelchairs and pushchairs). In the summer you can watch avocets and marsh harriers or hear booming bitterns. On the beach, a special area is cordoned off to protect nesting little terns. In the autumn and winter many wading birds and waterfowl visit the reserve. In the visitor centre you can find out more about the reserve and its wildlife, browse in the shop or enjoy a meal in the tearoom. There is a programme of events throughout the year, including special events for children and those new to birdwatching.

Opening times: reserve – 9 am to 9 pm or dusk if earlier (closed Tuesdays, 25 and 26 December); visitor centre – 9 am to 5 pm (4 pm winter).

non-members – adult £3.50, child 50p, concession £2.50, family ticket £7.

Little tern

M

Location: signposted from A12 and Westleton.
Map page 7.
Darsham (4 miles / 6.5 km;
nearest stop at Theberton (3 miles / 5 km), service twice daily.
☎ 01728 648281
i 01502 724729
Visitor centre
Nature trails 2 (about 2 miles / 3 km long), both partly wheelchair / pushchair accessible
Birdwatching hides 8 (5 wheelchair accessible, 3 can have cars parked nearby, by arrangement).

The hides overlooking The Scrape at Minsmere, give excellent views of many birds.

P Morecambe Bay, Lancashire

During migration and in winter, the reserve's sandflats and saltmarshes are vital feeding grounds for thousands of wading birds and wildfowl. At high tide, they are pushed back on to the saltmarshes, giving excellent birdwatching from Hest Bank (tide tables are available from Leighton Moss reserve). Do not go out onto the saltmarsh or intertidal area – there are dangerous channels and quicksands. Two coastal lagoons have been created close to Leighton Moss reserve, with nature trails and birdwatching hides.
Opening times: Hest Bank open at all times.
Location: Hest Bank foreshore is 2 miles/3 km north-east of Morecambe on the A5105. **Map** page 8.
≈ Morecambe for Hest Bank and Silverdale for other areas;
🚌 Hest Bank on approximately 2-hourly Morecambe to Carnforth service. See also Leighton Moss.
☎ 01524 701601
i 01524 582808
Nature trails to Eric Morecambe (wheelchair/pushchair accessible) and Allen Hides.

P Nagshead, Gloucestershire
T

Nagshead is famous for its breeding pied flycatchers. The nestboxes in which they nest have been monitored continuously since 1948. The wood is also home to hawfinches, buzzards and all three species of British woodpecker.
Opening times: reserve – open at all times.
Location: west of Parkend village, signposted off B4431 road to Coleford.
Map page 6.
≈ Lydney (6 miles/9.5 km) and Gloucester 22 miles/35 km;

🚌 Gloucester to Coleford service stops at Coalway, 2 miles/3 km from reserve
☎ 01594 562852
i 01665 576007
Information centre (seasonal)
Nature trails 2 (shortest 1 mile/1.5 km, wheelchair accessible in dry weather; longest 2.25 miles/3.5 km).
Birdwatching hides 2.

P Nor Marsh and Motney Hill, Kent

Nor Marsh is a saltmarsh island in the Medway Estuary. To the east is Motney Hill, another area of mud and saltmarsh. In the winter at both sites, large numbers of wildfowl can be seen, including brent geese, pintails, shelducks and goldeneyes along with grey plovers, knots and avocets. In the spring and autumn look out for black-tailed godwits. There are no RSPB run facilities, but there is a full range in the Riverside Country Park run by Gillingham Borough Council.
Opening times: 8.30 am to dusk.
Location: view from Riverside Country Park off B2004, 1 mile/1.6 km north of Gillingham. **Map** page 7.
≈ Rainham 2 miles/3 km, Gillingham 3 miles/5 km;
🚌 Twydall Shopping Centre (8 minutes from Gillingham).
☎ RSPB 01634 222480;
Riverside Country Park 01634 378987
i 01634 843666
Walks to view Nor Marsh 1 mile/1.6 km round trip (wheelchair and pushchair accessible), Motney Hill 3.5 miles/5.5 km round trip (pushchair accessible.)

P Northward Hill, Kent

Northward Hill is an excellent woodland for birds. As well as nightingales and turtle doves, the wood has the largest heronry in the UK, with over 200 pairs of grey herons nesting in the treetops. Wading bird such as lapwings and

M Read (RSPB Images)

In the winter, thousands of ducks and swans can be seen at the Ouse Washes.

redshanks breed. In the winter, wading birds and wildfowl including wigeons and teal can be seen, along with buzzards, hen harriers and merlins.

Opening times: public paths open at all times. Visits to other parts of the reserve (including the heronry) are by prior arrangement only.

用 use of trails and footpaths in public area is free. £2 for each non-member wishing to visit other parts of the reserve. Arrangements for special visits must be made in writing at least one month in advance.

Location: signposted from High Halstow, 4 miles/6.5 km north-east of Rochester.

Map page 7.

⇶ Strood (5 miles/8 km); 🚌 services from Strood stop regularly in High Halstow.

☎ 01634 222480
i 01634 843666

Nature trails 3 (shortest 0.3 mile/ 0.5 km, longest 2.5 miles;4 km, public footpath to marshes (4-mile/6.5-km round trip).

P Ouse Washes, Cambridgeshire

A visit to the Ouse Washes will give you an excellent introduction to the wildlife of the Fens. In the winter, the reserve floods. This attracts thousands of ducks and swans, which can be seen from the birdwatching hides along the banks. In the summer, wading birds such as redshanks and lapwings breed.

Opening times: birdwatching hides – always open; visitor centre – 9 am to 5 pm daily (closed 25 and 26 December).

用 non-members – £1 donation.

Location: signed from Manea village (2.5 miles/4 km) which is 6 miles/ 9.5 km east of Chatteris on the A142/A141 between Ely and March.

Map page 7.

⇶ Manea stop (3 miles/5 km), infrequent service.

☎ 01354 680212   *i* 01353 662062

Information centre
Birdwatching hides 10 (1 wheelchair accessible).

P

C H Gomersall (RSPB Images)

A misty winter morning at Pulborough Brooks

P Pulborough Brooks, West Sussex

In the scenic but easily accessible Arun valley, the RSPB has restored wet grassy meadows, which flood in winter. Controlled flooding gives a refuge to thousands of ducks, geese, swans and wading birds. Many breed in the summer, along with songbirds such as nightingales, and many colourful butterflies.

An attractive visitor centre is housed in a converted Sussex barn. Here begins a circular trail through hedge-lined lanes (2 miles/3 km maximum and suitable for pushchairs and manual wheelchairs with a strong helper).
Opening times: reserve – open daily (closed 25 December); visitor centre – open daily (closed 25 and 26 December) 10 am to 5 pm (tearoom closes 4.45 pm). non-members – adult £3, child £1, concession £1.50, family ticket £6.
Location: signposted on the A283 Pulborough to Storrington road, about

1 mile/1.6 km south of Pulborough.
Map page 7.
Pulborough (2 miles/3 km), taxi available.
☎ 01798 875851
i 01903 882268
Visitor centre
Nature trail – circular trail (2 miles/ 3 km) with shorter loops, suitable for most wheelchairs and pushchairs.
Birdwatching hides 4 (3 wheelchair accessible).
A batricar is available for free hire (advance booking recommended).

Wigeons

The visitor centre at Pulborough Brooks

R

P ⊞ Radipole Lake, Dorset

This reserve – situated in the centre of Weymouth – has plenty to offer to families and birdwatchers alike. The visitor centre has panoramic views of open water, and easy access to the rest of the reserve along firm paths suitable for wheelchairs and pushchairs. There is also an audio nature trail for the visually impaired.

The large reedbed, open water, flood meadows and scrub attract a good range of birds all year. The resident bearded tits and Cetti's warblers are joined in summer by reed, sedge and grasshopper warblers and in autumn by a variety of migrating birds calling in to rest and feed.
Opening times: visitor centre – daily 9 am to 5 pm; birdwatching hide – 8 am to dusk.

Radipole Lake

⊞ for use of hide, non-members – adult £2, child 50p, concession £1, family ticket £4.
Location: next to the Swannery Car Park in Weymouth. **Map** page 6.
⇌ Weymouth 430 yards / 393 m.
☎ 01305 778313
i 01305 785747
Public car park (reduced charge for RSPB members – show membership card)
Visitor centre
Nature trails (0.75–1.5 miles / 1.2–2.5 km)
Birdwatching hides 1, 1.5 miles / 2.5 km from visitor centre (wheelchair accessible).

Grey heron

P ⊞ Rutland Water, Rutland

This reserve, comprising Egleton and Lynden reserves, is run by the Leicestershire and Rutland Wildlife Trust in conjunction with Anglian Water. It is the site of the annual British Birdwatching Fair, of which the RSPB is a co-organiser.
The habitats include open water, lagoons, reedbeds, woodland, old meadows, hedgerows and grassland, attracts a wide range of birds.

Opening times: Egleton,
all year except Christmas and
Boxing day. Lynden, weekends
only in winter, daily except
Mondays in summer.
🏠 Charge for everyone.
Location: Egleton, 1mile /
1.5 km from Oakham off A6003
or A606. Lyndon,
1 mile / 1.5 km from Manton on
South Shore, Rutland Water.
🚆 Oakham Station
(2.5 miles / 4 km).
☎ 01572 770651
i 01780 460321
Nature trails
(wheelchair / pushchair
accessible)
Birdwatching hides 20
(10 wheelchair accessible by
April 1998).

J Halady (RSPB Images)

R

Kingfisher

P 🏠 🎏 👫 🚶 ♿ T Rye House Marsh, Hertfordshire

This small reserve is full of interest for
all the family. It is by the River Lea and
includes areas of reedbed, open water,
meadow and wood. In the summer, a
colony of common terns nests on
specially made rafts, while kingfishers
breed in artificial sandbanks. During the
winter, ducks such as shovelers,
gadwalls and tufted ducks can be seen
on the open water.
Opening times: 10 am to 5 pm daily.
🏠 non-members – adult £2, child 50p,
concession £1, family ticket £4.

Location: 2 miles / 3 km from A10 and
6 miles / 9.5 km north of M25 (J25) in
Hoddesdon. Follow signs for Rye Park
into Rye Road. **Map** page 7.
🚆 Rye House (300 yards / 275 m);
🚌 stop 500 yards / 457 m from reserve.
☎ 01992 460031
i 01992 584322
Nature trail (wheelchair / pushchair
accessible)
Birdwatching hides 5 (4 wheelchair
accessible). Information hide.

C H Gomersall (RSPB Images)

Rye House Marsh

Gadwall

C H Gomersall (RSPB Images)

Sandwell Valley is just a few miles from Birmingham.

P
S
T

Sandwell Valley, West Midlands

Just outside Birmingham and close to the M6, Sandwell Valley is enjoyable for all the family. In summer breeding birds around the marsh, lake and grassland range from wading birds such as little ringed plovers to ducks and songbirds such as whitethroats. Other birds visit on migration and in winter ducks and waders find refuge.

Opening times: reserve – open at all times; visitor centre – Tuesday to Friday 9 am to 5 pm; Saturday and Sunday 10 am to 5 pm.

Location: off Tanhouse Avenue via Hamstead Road in Great Barr.

Map page 7.

≥ Hamstead 2 miles/3 km;
frequent services from Birmingham and West Bromwich.

T Hamblin (RSPB Images)

Whitethroat

☎ 0121 358 3013
i 0121 693 6300
Visitor centre
Firm paths (suitable for wheelchairs and pushchairs)
Birdwatching hides 3 (2 wheelchair accessible).

Brent goose

P
Snettisham, Norfolk

Snettisham nature reserve is the place to see one of the country's greatest wildlife spectacles. As the tide rises and covers the Wash, hundreds of thousands of wading birds, ducks and geese gradually move up the beach and onto the reserve's pools. From the hides overlooking the pools you can watch the birds as they jostle for space. The best time to witness this spectacle is during the autumn and winter.

To get the most from your visit consult a tide table first. Tide tables are available from the RSPB East Anglia Office (01603 661662).

Opening times: open at all times.
Location: between King's Lynn and Hunstanton, signposted from the A149 at Snettisham. **Map** page 7.

≈ King's Lynn (13 miles / 21 km);
🚌 nearest stop 2 miles / 3 km, service every ½ hour from King's Lynn.
☎ 01485 542689
i 01485 532610
Nature trail about 3.5 miles / 5.5 km
Birdwatching hides 4
(disabled visitors can drive to the first hide).

Bar-tailed godwit

At high tide, thousands of wading birds cram on to the pits at Snettisham.

S

R Wilmshurst (RSPB Images)

Nightingales can be heard in the woods at Stour Estuary.

P Stour Estuary, Essex

At the Stour Estuary reserve you can enjoy both strolling through a coppiced wood and watching wading birds, ducks and geese on the estuary. In the spring, nightingales and other birds fill the woods with their songs. The flowers of spring are also particularly beautiful. To see estuary birds the best time to visit is during the autumn and winter.
Opening times: open at all times.
non-members – voluntary donation.
Location: 1 mile/1.6 km east of Wrabness on B1352 Manningtree to Harwich road. **Map** page 7.
Wrabness 0.5 mile/0.8 km;
buses from Colchester to Harwich via Wrabness pass the reserve car park.
☎ 01255 886043
i 01255 506139
Nature trails (shortest 1 mile/1.6 km – wheelchair/pushchair accessible during dry weather, longest 5 miles/8 km)
Birdwatching hides 3

P Strumpshaw Fen, Norfolk

Strumpshaw Fen is in the heart of the Norfolk Broads. A number of nature trails lead you through the varied habitats, including reedbeds and woodland. In the summer, there is a special trail in the flower-filled meadow. When walking near the reedbeds you may see a marsh harrier or see a swallowtail butterfly in the summer.
Opening times: daily – 9 am to 9 pm (dusk when earlier).
non-members – adult £2.50, child 50p, concession £1.50, family ticket £4.50.
Location: 0.75 mile/1.2 km SW of Strumpshaw and signposted from Brundall High Street off the A47 east of Norwich.
Map page 7.
Brundall (1.5 miles/2.5 km);
services from Norwich stop 0.5 mile/0.8 km from reserve on Brundall to Strumpshaw road.
☎ 01603 715191
i 01603 666071
Nature trails (shortest 1.5 miles/2.5 km, longest 3.25 miles/5 km). Information hide.
Birdwatching hides 4

R Revels (RSPB Images)

Swallowtail butterfly

C H Gomersall (RSPB Images)

Surlingham Church Marsh

P Symond's Yat,
Gloucestershire

The peregrine viewing point at Symond's Yat Rock is a joint project run by the RSPB and Forest Enterprise, who own the site. Between April and August, telescopes are set up to give close views of the nesting peregrines. The rock is a spectacular site high above the River Wye.

Opening times: daily, April to August.
Location: 3 miles north of Coleford on B4432, signposted from Forest Enterprise car park.
≈ Lydney (14 miles/22.5 km).
☎ 01594 562852
i 01665 576007

P Surlingham Church Marsh, Norfolk

Across the River Yare from Strumpshaw Fen, this is another Broadland reserve. A nature trail takes you around the edge of the reserve and from it you can see the birds of reed and sedge fen, ditches and open water.

Opening times: open at all times.
Location: Surlingham is 6 miles/9.5 km east of Norwich off the A146 Norwich to Lowestoft road.
Map page 7.
≈ Norwich (6 miles/9.5 km);
▥ infrequent service from Norwich to Surlingham.
☎ 01603 715191
i 01603 666071
Nature trail (1.25 miles/2 km)
Birdwatching hides 2

Peregrine

Sedge warbler

C Nicholson (RSPB Images)

Watching the peregrines at Symond's Yat.

33

T

C H Gomersall (RSPB Images)

Titchwell Marsh, home to breeding marsh harriers.

Titchwell Marsh, Norfolk

P
🏠
♦♦
☕
🍴
S
🔭
👪
🏃
♿

This wetland nature reserve is situated on the beautiful north Norfolk coast. A walk from the visitor centre down to the sandy beach takes you past reedbeds and shallow lagoons, each managed specially for birds. In the summer, marsh harriers can be seen hunting over the reeds. Winter sees the arrival of many birds such as ducks and geese. The well-stocked shop has a wide range of RSPB gifts, books and souvenirs. The two hides and the paths are suitable for those in wheelchairs.

Opening times: reserve – open at all times; visitor centre and shop – daily 10 am to 5 pm (4 pm November to March), closed 25 and 26 December.
🏠 non-members – £3 per car (£5 per mini-bus).

Location: 5 miles/8 km east of Hunstanton on the A149. **Map** page 7.
≽ King's Lynn (21 miles/38 km);
🚌 from Hunstanton and Wells-next-the-Sea (request stop at reserve entrance).
☎ 01485 210779
i 01485 532610
Visitor centre
Firm path to beach with 2 gentle slopes (wheelchair/pushchair accessible).

G Downey (RSPB Images)

Bearded tit

P Tudeley Woods, Kent

All three British species of woodpecker live in the wood as well as nuthatches and treecreepers. The springtime carpet of bluebells and primroses is an impressive sight. This is also a good time to listen to the songs of the many different warblers that nest on the reserve. In the summer look out for orchids and butterflies, including the white admiral and speckled wood.
Opening times: open at all times.
Location: near to the A21 Tonbridge to Hastings road, off the minor road to Capel, 2 miles/3 km south of Tonbridge.
Map page 7.
⇌ Tonbridge (3 miles/5 km).
☎ 01273 775333
i 01892 515675
Nature trails 2 (0.75 and 1.25 miles/ 1.2 and 2 km) – the trails can be very muddy after rain and during the winter.

E A Janes (RSPB Images)

Brimstone butterfly

P West Sedgemoor, Somerset

The Somerset Levels and Moors are one of England's largest remaining wet meadow systems. Large numbers of wading birds breed here and the winter floods attract Bewick's swans, teals, wigeons and lapwings. Swell Wood, an ancient deciduous wood on the southern edge of the reserve, has one of the UK's largest heronries, which is best visited between March and June.
Opening times: open at all times.
Location: car park is signposted just off the A378 Taunton – Langport road, 1 mile/1.6 km east of Fivehead.
Map page 6.
⇌ Taunton 11 miles/18 km;
🚌 stop in Fivehead on A378 – Southern National Taunton to Yeovil service.
☎ 01458 252805
i 01823 336344
Nature trail 0.5/0.8 km woodland trail
Birdwatching hides 2 (Swell Wood hide wheelchair accessible).

P Wolves Wood, Suffolk

This reserve is one of the few remaining areas of the ancient woodland that used to cover East Anglia. The RSPB is continuing the traditional coppicing method of managing it, which means the wood has a wide variety of birds, plants and mammals. In the spring it is a good place to hear the beautiful song of the nightingale.
Opening times: open at all times.
Location: 2 miles/3 km east of Hadleigh on the A1071 to Ipswich.
Map page 7.
🚌 nearest stop Hadleigh, hourly services from Ipswich.
☎ 01255 886043
i 01473 258070
Nature trail (1 mile/1.6 km)
Birdwatching hides 1

T-V

Northern Ireland

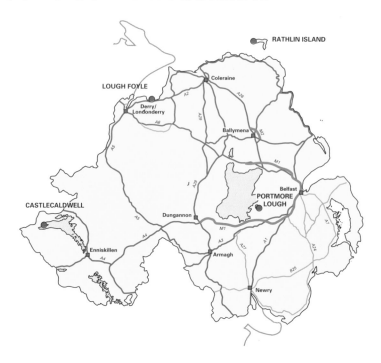

P Castlecaldwell Forest and Lower Lough Erne Islands, County Fermanagh

The reserve is a mix of coniferous forest and 40 diverse islands in Lower Lough Erne. The breeding birds of the reserve include snipe, redshanks, curlews and Sandwich terns. In winter, whooper swans and geese can be found.

Opening times: forest open at all times. Lusty More is the only island open to the public – access by boat only.

Location: The forest is 7 miles/11 km east of Belleek off the A47 to Kesh.

☎ 013656 658358.

i 01365 323110

Nature trails from car park (up to 2 miles/3 km) long. One short trail on Lusty More Island.

Birdwatching hides 2

Lough Foyle, County Londonderry

Various viewpoints give excellent views over the mudflats and adjacent fields. In early winter, the Lough is an outstanding place to see large numbers of waterfowl, including brent geese, whooper swans and wigeons.

Opening times: open at all times.

Location: the reserve can be accessed via a number of minor roads off the A2 between Limavady and Londonderry.

 Londonderry (8 miles/13 km);

 Ballykelly.

☎ 01232 491547

i 01504 722226

Portmore Lough, County Antrim

The reserve lies on the southern shore of Portmore Lough on the east side of Lough Neagh. There is wet grassland fringed by woodland and scrub. In the winter greylag geese and whooper swans visit the fields. In the summer lapwings, snipe and wildfowl can be found. Visitor facilities are planned for 1997-98.

Opening times: Please contact the warden to arrange a visit.

Location: Leave M1 at J9 to Aghalee then follow Ballycairn road to Gawley's Gate and turn right. George's Island road is about 1 mile on the right.

🚆 Ballinderry;

☎ 01846 652406.

Razorbill

Rathlin Island Cliffs, County Antrim

Rathlin Island is five miles off the north coast of Northern Ireland. From late May to early July, the spectacular cliffs on the reserve are home to thousands of breeding seabirds. The West Light platform gives magnificent views of guillemots, razorbills, puffins and fulmars.

Opening times: April to August. Visitors must contact the warden first.

Location: Rathlin Island is five miles off the coast from Ballycastle. The West Light platform is about 4 miles from the harbour.

🚆 Ballymoney (15 miles/24 km);

🚢 from Ballycastle April and May 10 am and June to August 9.15 am and 11.15 am;

🚐 mini-bus on island to West Light.

☎ 012657 63948.

i 01265 762024

Facilities: the West Light platform offers excellent, safe views of the seabird colony. Access is only under the supervision of wardening staff.

P-R

Robert Thompson

The cliffs on Rathlin Island are crammed with breeding seabirds in the spring and early summer.

Scotland

FORSINARD

Ullapool

BALRANALD

UDALE BAY

Cromarty

Lochmaddy

Uig

Nairn

CUL
SAI

Kyle of
Lochalsh

Inverness

LOCH
RUTHVEN

Aviemore

Kingussie

INSH
MARSHE

Mallaig

Invergarry

GLENBORRODALE

Fort William

KILLIECRAN

Arinagour

COLL

INVERSNAID

B8079

LOCH
GRUINART

Crianlarich

Oban

Callander

Dunferm

Greenock

LOCHWINNOCH

Glasgow

Motherw

Port Askaig

Kennacraig

BARC
HAU

Hamilton

Port Ellen

Ayr

KEN-DEE
MARSHES

Girvan

WOOD
OF CREE

Dumfries

Newton
Stewart

Stranraer

MERSEHEAI

Drummore

MULL OF
GALLOWAY

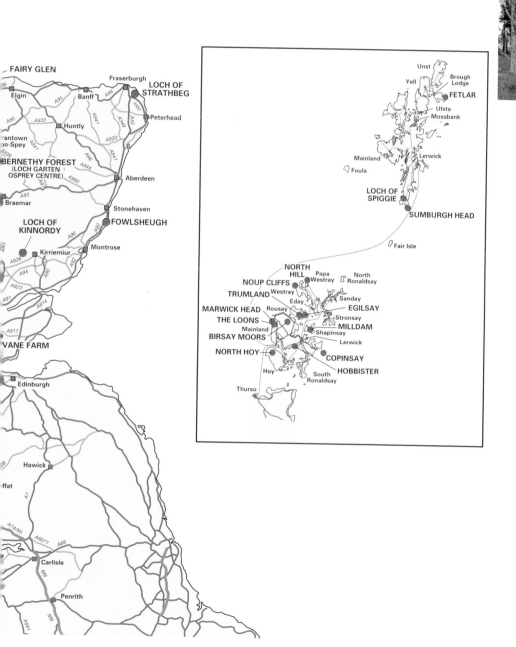

C H Gomersall (RSPB Images)

Loch Mallachie, in the Abernethy Forest Nature Reserve.

Abernethy Forest – Loch Garten, Highland

C H Gomersall (RSPB Images)

Loch Garten is famous for the ospreys which can be seen from the Osprey Centre in summer. As well as an excellent view of the nest, live video pictures are relayed back to the Centre, where staff are on hand to explain what is happening. The walk from the car park to the Centre takes you through Caledonian pine forest, now a rare habitat. You may see crested tits, Scottish crossbills or red squirrels on this walk or on one of the other three trails around the reserve.

Opening times: reserve – open at all times. Osprey Centre – daily from late April to the end of August, 10 am to 6 pm.

Admission charge to the Osprey Centre: non-members – adult £2, child 50p, concession £1, family ticket £4.

Osprey

Mark Hamblin (RSPB Images)

Watching live TV pictures of the osprey nest.

Location: 10 miles/16 km east of Aviemore between the villages of Boat of Garten and Nethybridge off the B970. Follow the RSPB osprey signs (spring and summer only).

≈ Aviemore 10 miles/16 km;

🚍 nearest stop 1.5 miles/2.5 km from Osprey Centre, daily services from Aviemore to Nethybridge.

☎ 01479 831694

i 01479 810363

Visitor centre (wheelchair accessible)

Nature trails 3 (shortest 1.5 miles/ 2.5 km, longest 4 miles/6.5 km) the shortest is suitable for wheelchair users (with a strong helper) and pushchairs. Guided walks and events in summer.

Red squirrel

P Balranald, North Uist, Western Isles

Sandy beaches and a rocky foreshore are separated from the machair and marshes by sand dunes; there are also shallow lochs. The information centre explains the importance of traditional crofting agriculture for the now rare corncrake and other wildlife. Many species of wading birds nest on the flower-rich machair and the croftland.

Opening times: reserve – open at all times; visitor centre – April to August, 9 am to 6 pm.

Location: 3 miles/5 km north of Bayhead. Turn for Hougharry off the A865.

🚍 post bus service; ⚓ nearest port Lochmaddy; ✈ Glasgow.

☎ 01870 620369

i 01876 500321

Information centre at Goular Cottage

Nature trail (3.5 miles/5.5 km) which is unsuitable for wheelchairs.

P Baron's Haugh, North Lanarkshire

On a walk around this small urban nature reserve you will find a meadow, some marshland, woodland and the River Clyde. This diversity of habitats makes it valuable for wildlife and over 170 species of birds have been recorded here. You may see kingfishers by the river and whooper swans on the flooded meadows (haugh) in the winter.

Opening times: open at all times.

Location: to the south of Motherwell, close to the M74 (J4).

≈ Motherwell and Airbles Road;

🚍 Airbles Road.

☎ 01505 842663

i 01698 267676

Nature trails 2 (0.5 mile/0.8 km and 2 miles/3 km). The longer trail is suitable for wheelchairs and pushchairs.

Birdwatching hides 4 (2 wheelchair accessible and can be reached by car).

B

P Birsay Moors and Cottasgarth, Orkney

In the summer hen harriers, short-eared owls and arctic skuas nest on the moorland. The Orkney vole is also common on the reserve.
Opening times: open at all times.
Location: 5 miles/8 km north of Finstown off the A966.
🦗 contact P&O Ferries 01224 572615;
✈ flights from Edinburgh.
☎ 01856 721210
i 01856 872856
Birdwatching hides 2

R T Smith (RSPB Images)

Corncrake

P Coll, Argyll and Bute

🏃 Our reserve on the island of Coll has long, white shell beaches, sand dunes and machair grassland, all typical Hebridean habitats. The reserve is a stronghold for the rare corncrake. We are managing the reserve with local farmers to help corncrake numbers recover. There are also many other breeding birds on the reserve including redshanks, lapwings and snipe. In the winter large numbers of barnacle and Greenland white-fronted geese use the site.
Opening times: open at all times. Please avoid walking through fields of hay and crops.

Location: 6 miles/9.5 km west of Arinagour, Isle of Coll.
Public transport: Coll is reached by ferry from Oban.
☎ 01879 230301
i 01688 302182
Information bothy at Totronald. Guided walks in summer.

Copinsay, Orkney

This uninhabited island was purchased as a memorial to the naturalist James Fisher. The cliffs of the reserve are home to a huge colony of breeding seabirds, including fulmars, guillemots, razorbills and kittiwakes.
Opening times: open at all times, weather permitting.
Location: 2 miles/3 km off the east coast of East Mainland.
🦗 day trips by boat from Skaill, contact S Foubister on 01856 741252.
✈ flights from Edinburgh.
☎ 01856 721210
i 01856 872856
Facilities: Old farmhouse on island may be available for basic overnight accommodation. For more information please telephone 01856 721210.

P Culbin Sands, Highland

Overlooking the Moray Firth, Culbin Sands forms one of the largest shingle and sand dune bars in Britain, behind which there is extensive saltmarsh. Large numbers of sea ducks can be seen offshore during the winter. Bar-tailed godwits, oystercatchers and knots flock at high tide. Much of the reserve is remote, unspoilt and largely undisturbed.
Opening times: open at all times.
Location: 1.5 miles/2.5 km east of Nairn off the Lochloy road.
🚂 and 🚌 Nairn 1.5 miles/2.5 km.
☎ 01540 661518
i 01667 452753

B-C

Egilsay, Orkney

This reserve was acquired in 1996 mainly for breeding corncrakes. Our management of the reserve will create the ideal conditions for them when they arrive from Africa in the spring.

Opening times: open at all times, but please contact the warden before your visit.

Location: 1 mile/1.6 km off coast of Rousay

🚢 service from Tingwall, contact Orkney Ferries, tel: 01856 751360.

☎ 01856 821395

i 01856 872856

P Fetlar, Shetland

During the summer, a wealth of birds breed on the reserve, including 90% of the British population of red-necked phalaropes. These fascinating waders can be seen from the RSPB hide or at the Loch of Funzie. Red-throated divers, whimbrels, and arctic and great skuas also breed on the island.

Opening times: hide open April to October; no access to the statutory bird sanctuary April to August.

Location: via ferry from Yell/Unst.

🚢 contact P&O Ferries 01224 572615;

✈ flights from Edinburgh, Inverness, Aberdeen.

☎ 01957 733246

i 01595 693434

Facilities: Fetlar Interpretative Centre, has an RSPB display. Public toilets at ferry terminal.

Birdwatching hide 1 at Mires of Funzie.

Red-necked phalarope

P Forsinard, Highland

Comprising almost 17,300 acres/7,000 ha of 'blanket bog', the deep peatlands of Forsinard lie at the heart of the internationally important Flow Country of Caithness and Sutherland. Birds including golden plovers, dunlins and merlins breed on the reserve. We are conserving the bogs while encouraging limited access via our visitor centre at Forsinard railway station, a bog pool trail, regular guided walks and road-side viewing.

Opening times: visitor centre open daily, 9 am to 6 pm, April to October.

🎫 free, but donations welcome.

Location: on the A897 14 miles/22.5 km from Helmsdale.

🚆 Forsinard station.

☎ 01641 571225

i 01955 602596

Visitor centre at Forsinard station (wheelchair accessible)

Nature trail (1 mile/1.6 km).

P Fowlsheugh, Grampian

The cliffs of Fowlsheugh reserve are packed with breeding seabirds in the spring and summer. Guillemots, razorbills and kittiwakes breed in large numbers, with smaller numbers of fulmars, herring gulls, puffins and shags. In May and June, boat trips from Stonehaven visit the cliffs in the evening to watch the nesting seabirds. Details from the number below.

Opening times: open at all times.

Location: 3 miles/5 km south of Stonehaven, the car park at Crawton is signposted off the A92.

🚆 Stonehaven 3 miles/5 km;

🚌 request stop at Crawton turn-off.

☎ 01224 624824

i 01569 762806

Please take care along the cliff top path.

E-F

✗ Glenborrodale, Highland

On the rugged Ardnamurchan peninsula, Glenborrodale is an ancient oak wood on the north shore of Loch Sunart. In spring, wood warblers nest, along with a range of woodland birds such as redstarts and spotted flycatchers. There is always a good chance of seeing an otter along the shore and seals are common.

G-I

Opening times: open at all times.
Location: 1 mile/1.6 km west of Glenborrodale on the B8007.
☎ 01540 661518
i 01397 703781
Nature trail (2 miles/3 km)
Guided walks in summer from Glenmore Natural History Centre.

P Hobbister, Orkney

The reserve is a mixture of moorland, sandflats, saltmarsh and sea cliffs. Hen harriers, short-eared owls and red-throated divers breed on the moorland. On the coast look out for red-breasted mergansers and black guillemots.
Opening times: open at all times, but access is limited to the land between the A964 and the sea.
Location: 4 miles south-west of Kirkwall.
🚢 contact P&O Ferries 01224 572615;
✈ flights from Edinburgh.
☎ 01856 721210
i 01856 872856

Red-breasted mergansers

P Inner Clyde, West Dunbarton

The Finlaystone reserve is an area of mudflats on the south side of this important estuary. In the winter there are lots of wildfowl and wading birds to see including goldeneyes, red-breasted mergansers, eiders, redshanks and greenshanks.
Opening times: open at all times.
Location: 1.5 miles/2.5 km east of Port Glasgow, access from roundabout on A8 to Parklea. Also slip road to West Ferry 4 miles/6.5 km east of Port Glasgow.
🚆 Port Glasgow 1.5 miles/2.5 km from Parklea;
🚌 services every 20 minutes to Port Glasgow, 1.5 miles/2.5 km from Parklea.
☎ 01505 842663
i 01475 639467
Viewpoints from Parklea and West Ferry, and from the footpath along the edge of Parklea playing field.

P Insh Marshes, Highland
⛱ 👪 ✗

This is one of the most important wetlands in Europe. In spring, lapwings, redshanks and curlews nest here. In winter the marshes flood, providing roosting and feeding for flocks of whooper swans and greylag geese. The best time for visiting is between November and June.
Opening times: open at all times.
Location: 1.5 miles/2.5 km from Kingussie on the B970.
🚆 Kingussie 1.5 miles/2.5 km;
🚌 frequent services from Inverness and Perth stop in Kingussie.
☎ 01540 661518 or 01540 662332
i 01540 661297
Information viewpoint
Nature trails 2 (2 miles/3 km and 2.5 miles/4 km) Due to the rocky terrain, neither are accessible to wheelchairs or pushchairs, but there are good views of the reserve from the B970.
Birdwatching hides 2

D Kjaer (RSPB Images)

Redstart

P Ken-Dee Marshes, Dumfries and Galloway

The reserve is both a wetland and woodland site. In the winter, many wildfowl, including white-fronted geese, can be seen on the reserve. During the spring, migrant redstarts and pied flycatchers join the resident woodland birds to breed. Red squirrels and otters are also found on the reserve.
Opening times: open at all times.
Location: car park on minor road north from Glenlochar to the A762.
Public transport: none.
☎ 01671 402861
i 01556 502611
Nature trail (3 miles/5 km)
Birdwatching hides 1

I-K

P Inversnaid, Stirling
⚭

Inversnaid is set on the east shore of Loch Lomond. The woodland rises steeply from the shores of the loch and then gives way to open moorland. In the summer, pied flycatchers and redstarts breed here, along with resident birds. Buzzards nest on the crags in the wood and black grouse can sometimes be seen on the moorland.

There is a path through the woodland, but it is steep and rugged in places and is therefore not suitable for pushchairs or those with limited mobility.
Opening times: open at all times.
Location: 15 miles/24 km west of Aberfoyle at the end of the B829 and an unclassified road.
⇝ Stirling 35 miles/56 km;
🚌 daily post buses from Aberfoyle and minibuses from Callander and Aberfoyle. Bus stop at Inversnaid Hotel is about 0.5 mile/0.8 km from the reserve.
☎ 0141 945 5224
i 01877 382352
Nature trail (1 mile/1.6 km)
Toilets March to October only.

P Killiecrankie, Tayside

Rising from the dramatic narrow gorge of the River Garry, the reserve climbs steeply through oak and birch woodland to heather moorland. There is a great variety of woodland and moorland birds including buzzards, redstarts, curlews and black and red grouse. Ravens nest on the crags.

The reserve is exceptionally rich in plant life, with a number of rare and unusual species, but also a colourful show of common plants throughout the spring and summer.
Opening times: open at all times.
🅿 non-members – £1 parking fee.
Location: 4 miles/6.5 km NW of Pitlochry on the B8097, signposted from Killiecrankie on unclassified roads to Balrobbie Farm.
⇝ Pitlochry 4 miles/6.5 km;
🚌 Killiecrankie.
☎ 01577 862355
i 01796 472215
Nature trails 2 (1.5 miles/2.5 km and 3 miles/5 km) both of which are steep and rough and unsuitable for wheelchairs or pushchairs.

L

Barnacle geese at Loch Gruinart

P Loch Gruinart, Islay, Argyll and Bute

During the spring there are hundreds of breeding waders (lapwings, redshanks and snipe) and the nights resound to the call of the corncrake. Hen harriers nest on the moor and hunting golden eagles and peregrines occur all year round.

Loch Gruinart is famous for the large numbers of barnacle and white-fronted geese that spend the winter on Islay. The reserve can be seen easily from the road, letting you birdwatch from a car. In the visitor centre a live video camera lets you get even closer views of the grazing geese.
Opening times: visitor centre – April to October 10 am to 5 pm, November to March 10 am to 4 pm (closed 26 December and 1 January).
Location: signed from A847 Bridgend to Bruichladdich road, 3 miles/5 km from turn off.
⏀ from Kennacraig to Port Askaig or Port Ellen; ✈ from Glasgow to Islay; 🚌 nearest stop 3 miles/5 km.
☎ 01496 850505
i 01496 810254
Visitor centre
Birdwatching hides 1

P 🖰 Loch of Kinnordy, Angus

The lochs, mires and fens of the reserve are surrounded by farmland. It is one of the best places in Scotland for seeing black-necked grebes, which nest in the midst of a colony of black-headed gulls. Ospreys visit regularly in the summer.
Opening times: daily 9 am to dusk (closed Saturdays in September and October).
🖰 non-members – £1 parking fee.
Location: 1 mile/1.6 km west of Kirriemuir on the B951.
🚃 Dundee; 🚌 frequent services from Dundee and Forfar to Kirriemuir.
☎ 01575 574553 (summer only), 01224 624824 at other times
i 01575 574097
Nature trail and boardwalk to Swamp Hide (wheelchair accessible)
Birdwatching hides 3

Osprey

P Loch Ruthven, Highland

This beautiful loch is fringed by sedges and birch woods with open moorland. It is the most important site in the UK for the rare Slavonian grebe. The hide provides the perfect setting to watch the grebes without causing disturbance. Ospreys and black grouse can be seen regularly and there is also a chance of seeing a peregrine or hen harrier.
Opening times: open at all times.
Location: 11 miles/18 km south-west of Inverness, reached via the A9 and B851 taking the turn at East Croachy.
≈ Inverness 11 miles/18 km;
🚌 services twice daily to East Croachy, 1 mile/1.6 km from reserve.
☎ 01540 661518
_i_ 01463 234353
Birdwatching hides 1

M Hunt (RSPB Images)

Slavonian grebe

P Loch of Spiggie, Mainland, Shetland

The large shallow loch attracts large numbers of wildfowl during the autumn and winter, including whooper swans, wigeons and teals. In the summer arctic terns, arctic and great skuas and kittiwakes can be seen bathing in the loch.

Opening times: no access to reserve, but good views of loch from road.
Location: 2 miles/3 km north of Sumburgh Airport, turn off the B9122 near Scousburgh.
🚢 contact P&O Ferries 01224 572615;
✈ flights from Edinburgh;
🚌 daily service between Lerwick and Sumburgh.
☎ 01950 460800
_i_ 01595 693434

P Loch of Strathbeg, Aberdeenshire

This wetland reserve is an excellent place to see pink-footed geese and whooper swans during the winter. In the summer the meadows attract breeding wading birds, including lapwings and redshanks. On the small islands in the loch, Sandwich and common terns and a variety of wildfowl breed. The visitor centre observation room offers a panoramic view of the reserve.
Opening times: open at all times.
🏠 non-members – adult £1, child 50p, family ticket £2.50.
Location: signposted from the A952 at Crimond.
≈ Aberdeen 40 miles/64 km;
🚌 regular services from Peterhead and Fraserburgh stop at Crimond village (1 mile/1.6 km from visitor centre). Access to the whole reserve is difficult without a vehicle (4 miles/6.5 km from centre to hide).
☎ 01346 532017
Visitor centre with observation room
Nature trail short trail between hides
Birdwatching hides 4 (1 wheelchair accessible).

Sandwich tern

L

Doug Corrance (Still Moving Images)

Lochwinnoch

P
🚲
🏠

🚻 ☕ 🪑 S 🔭 🚻 🚶 ♿

Lochwinnoch, Renfrewshire

Situated within the Clyde-Muirshiel Regional Park, Lochwinnoch is one of the few remaining wetland sites in west Scotland. The visitor centre, with its viewing tower and telescopes, gives good views over the marshland and loch, where in the winter you may see whooper swans, greylag geese and goosanders.

In the spring, great crested grebes and lapwings can be seen displaying and sedge warblers can be heard singing in the marshland. Otters are occasionally seen.

The reserve is ideal for all the family as the trails, birdwatching hides and visitor centre are easily accessible. A programme of events is run throughout the year. While in the centre you can enjoy a light snack or browse in the RSPB shop.

Opening times: daily 10 am to 5 pm (closed 25 December and 1 January).
🏠 non-members – adult £2, child 50p, concession £1, family ticket £4.
Location: the reserve is 18 miles / 29 km south-west of Glasgow between Paisley and Largs on the A760 near Lochwinnoch.
🚃 Lochwinnoch (opposite reserve);
🚌 request stop outside reserve, regular services from Glasgow.
☎ 01505 842663
i 0141 889 0711
Visitor centre
Nature trails 2 (0.25 mile / 0.4 km and 0.5 mile / 0.8 km) both suitable for wheelchairs and pushchairs
Birdwatching hides 4 (3 wheelchair accessible).

Greylag goose

Great crested grebes breed at Lochwinnoch.

P The Loons, Orkney

This marshland reserve is one of the best remaining marshes in the Orkney islands. In the summer pintails and waders breed, while in the winter, the flooded marsh attracts hundreds of ducks and smaller numbers of white-fronted geese.
Opening times: there is no access to the marsh, but good views can be obtained from the road and hide.
Location: 3 miles/5 km north of Dounby on Orkney Mainland.
🚢 contact P&O Ferries 01224 572615;
✈ flights from Edinburgh.
☎ 01856 721210
i 01856 872856
Birdwatching hide 1

P Marwick Head, Orkney

The reserve is in the north-west corner of the Mainland. Thousands of pairs of seabirds crowd onto the cliffs. The cliff top has spectacular displays of sea campion, thrift and spring squill.
Opening times: open at all times.
Location: About 11 miles north of Stromness.
🚢 contact P&O Ferries 01224 572615;
✈ flights from Edinburgh.
☎ 01856 721210
i 01856 872856

P Mersehead, Dumfries and Galloway

Mersehead is an exciting new reserve covering a large area of farmland, wet meadows, saltmarsh and mudflats on the north shore of the Solway. It is important for wintering wildfowl including barnacle geese, pink-footed geese, wigeons and pintails. We are managing the reserve to encourage lapwings, curlews, redshanks and waterfowl to breed here. We are also planning to create a reedbed.

Opening times: open at all times.
🏠 Donations welcome.
Location: 18 miles/29 km south-west of Dumfries on the A710 just before Caulkerbush. First turn on left after Southwick Home Farm.
🚌 daily rural service from Dumfries stops one mile from reserve on A710.
☎ 01387 780298
i 01387 253862
Nature trails 2 (1.5 miles/2.5 km and 3.5 miles/5.5 km)
Birdwatching hide 1, (Information Centre scheduled to open in 1997).

L-M

R Wilmshurst (RSPB Images)

Shoveler

P Mill Dam, Shapinsay, Orkney

In winter, whooper swans can often be seen on the reserve along with greylag geese. In the summer pintails breed on the marsh with other ducks including wigeons and shovelers.
Opening times: hide open at all times, but no access to the reserve.
Location: 1 mile/1.5 km north-east of Balfour village
🚢 from Kirkwall, contact Orkney Ferries tel: 01856 872044.
☎ 01856 711373
i 01856 872856
Birdwatching hide 1 (wheelchair accessible).

P ⚓ Mull of Galloway, Dumfries and Galloway

The Mull of Galloway is the most southerly point in Scotland. From the cliffs you get excellent views over the Solway Firth and Irish Sea to the Isle of Man. The cliffs are home to thousands of breeding seabirds including guillemots, razorbills and a few puffins. The best time of year to watch the nesting seabirds is between April and July. On the small rocky outcrop, Scare Rocks, RSPB reserve, over 2,000 pairs of gannets breed.
Opening times: open at all times. The seasonal information point is usually open from mid-May to mid-July, 10.30 am to 5 pm Tuesdays to Sundays. Please check times before your visit.
🏠 free, but donations welcome.
Location: 5 miles/8 km south of Drummore and well signposted.
🚌 daily services from Drummore.
☎ 01671 402861
i 01776 702595
There is a variety of short cliff-top walks, but please take care on the cliff tops. Guided walks May to August only.

North Hill, Papa Westray, Orkney

The low cliffs are home to breeding seabirds, including guillemots, razorbills and kittiwakes. On the hill, a large colony of arctic terns nests close to arctic skuas, eiders, ringed plovers and oystercatchers.
Opening times: open at all times. During the breeding season, please contact the summer warden before visiting.
Location: on northern part of Papa Westray.
⚓ from Kirkwall, contact Orkney Ferries tel 01856 872044;
✈ flights from Kirkwall, contact Loganair tel 01856 872494.
☎ 01857 644240 (April to August only)
i 01856 872856

P North Hoy, Orkney

The reserve is a mixture of moorland and cliffs and includes the famous Old Man of Hoy rock stack. Great skuas breed on the moor along with red grouse, dunlins and golden plovers. Seabirds, including guillemots, razorbills and kittiwakes, breed on the cliffs.
Opening times: open at all times.
Location: on north-west part of Hoy.
⚓ daily service from Stromness to Moness Pier or Houton to Lyness service.
☎ 01856 791298
i 01856 872856

Great skua

The cliffs at Hoy and the Old Man of Hoy.

C H Gomersall (RSPB Images)

Guillemot

P Noup Cliffs, Westray, Orkney

These isolated cliffs have one of the UK's largest seabird colonies. On the 1.5 mile/2.5 km stretch of cliffs, over 44,500 guillemots and 12,700 pairs of kittiwakes breed, along with razorbills and fulmars.
Opening times: open at all times.
Location: from Pierowall follow the minor road west to Noup Farm, then the track to the lighthouse at the north end of the reserve.
🚢 from Kirkwall, contact Orkney Ferries 01856 872044.
☎ 01857 644240 (April to August only)
i 01856 872856

P 𝒳 Sumburgh Head, Mainland, Shetland

The cliffs around Sumburgh Head attract thousands of breeding seabirds including puffins, guillemots, shags and fulmars. Gannets are regularly seen off-shore; a number of whales and dolphins can also sometimes be seen.
Opening times: the reserve is always open.
Location: southern most tip of Mainland Shetland, 2.25 miles/3.5 km from Sumburgh Airport.
🚢 contact P&O Ferries 01224 572615;
✈ flights from Edinburgh.
🚌 daily service from Lerwick to Sumburgh Airport and Grutness.
☎ 01950 460800
i 01595 693434

P Trumland, Rousay, Orkney

Red-throated divers, merlins and hen harriers all breed on the heather moorland of this reserve.
Opening times: open at all times.
Location: near Trumland House in the south of Rousay.
🚢 from Tingwall, contact Orkney Ferries tel 01856 872044.
☎ 01856 821395
i 01856 872856
Nature trail 1

Otter

P Udale Bay, Highland

Udale Bay is an extensive area of mudflat, saltmarsh and wet grassland on the Cromarty Firth. From late summer to April the reserve supports large numbers of wildfowl and wading birds. Best visited within an hour of the high tide, there can be spectacular views of flocks of wading birds. In autumn up to 5,000 wigeons feed on the beds of eel-grass that grow in the Bay. Late summer is a good time to see fishing ospreys.
Opening times: open at all times.
Location: 1 mile/1.6 km west of Jemimaville on the B9163.
🚆 Dingwall 16 miles/26 km;
🚌 Jemimaville 4 times a day.
☎ 01540 661518
i 01463 234353
Birdwatching hides 1 (wheelchair accessible).

Vane Farm in winter

Vane Farm, Perthshire and Kinross

P

This 'gateway to the North' is one of the most popular RSPB nature reserves in Scotland. The visitor centre overlooks the loch where greylag and pink-footed geese, whooper swans and thousands of dabbling ducks spend the winter. The wet grassland is managed for nesting redshanks, snipe, lapwings and ducks.

One trail leads visitors to hides overlooking the floods and loch. The second, longer nature trail guides visitors through woodland to the spectacular view from the top of Vane Hill. A summer walk often gives views of willow warblers, tree pipits and perhaps great spotted woodpeckers.
Opening times: centre daily, 10 am to 5 pm April to December, 10 am to 4 pm January to March.
non-members – adult £2, child 50p, concession £1, family ticket £4.
Location: on the south shore of Loch Leven, 1 mile/1.6 km along the B9097 east of M90 (J5) (signposted from the motorway).
Lochgelly 4 miles/6.5 km, Cowdenbeath 4 miles/6.5 km; the nearest stops are in Kinross 6 miles/9.5 km and Ballingry 5 miles/ 8 km.

Pink-footed geese

R Wilmshurst (RSPB Images)

Lapwing

V-W

☎ 01577 862355
i 01577 863680
Visitor centre
Nature trails 2 (shortest 0.5 mile/ 0.8 km, longest 1 mile/1.6 km)
Birdwatching hides 3 plus observation room in visitor centre, which is wheelchair accessible.

Wood of Cree, Dumfries and Galloway

P

The Wood of Cree is the largest ancient wood in southern Scotland. In spring, the wood is alive with the sound of bird song, as the resident birds are joined by redstarts, pied flycatchers and garden warblers from Africa.
Opening times: open at all times.
free, but donations welcome.
Location: 3 miles/5 km north of Minnigaff/Newton Stewart on the east bank of the river Cree. Follow signs through Old Minnigaff.
Public transport:
Newton Stewart 3 miles/5 km.
☎ 01671 402861
i 01671 402431
Nature trail (1 mile/1.6 km with a 1 mile/1.6 km extension).

Ramsey Island

Wales

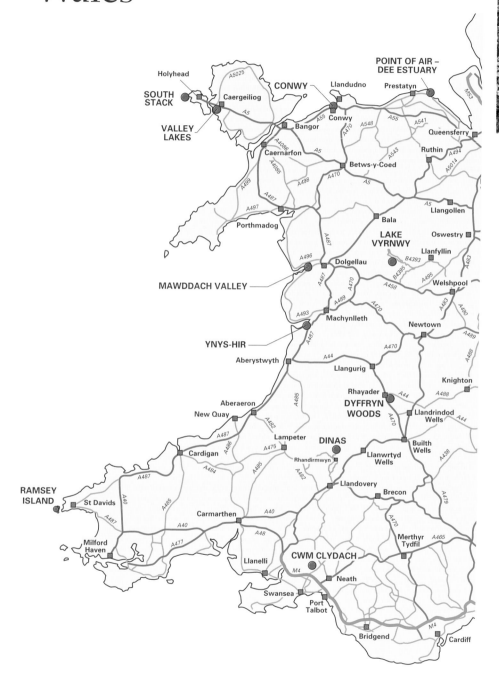

Holyhead

A5025

POINT OF AIR –
DEE ESTUARY

CONWY

Llandudno

Prestatyn

SOUTH
STACK

Caergeiliog

Conwy

A55

A55

A541

M53

VALLEY
LAKES

A5

Bangor

A548

Queensferry

A5

A470

A543

Ruthin

A494

Caernarfon

A4086

A5

Betws-y-Coed

A5014

A4085

A498

A470

A5

A499

A497

A5

Llangollen

A487

Porthmadog

Bala

Oswestry

LAKE
VYRNWY

A487

Llanfyllin

A483

Dolgellau

B4395

A496

B4393

Welshpool

MAWDDACH VALLEY

A487

A470

A458

A495

A483

A490

A489

A470

A493

Machynlleth

Newtown

A489

YNYS-HIR

A487

A44

A470

A468

Aberystwyth

Llangurig

Knighton

A485

Rhayader

A44

A488

Aberaeron

DYFFRYN
WOODS

Llandrindod
Wells

New Quay

A482

A470

A44

A487

Lampeter

DINAS

Builth
Wells

Cardigan

A496

A475

Rhandirmwyn

Llanwrtyd
Wells

A438

A485

A485

A462

RAMSEY
ISLAND

A484

Llandovery

Brecon

A479

St Davids

A487

A485

Carmarthen

A40

A470

A40

A48

Merthyr
Tydfil

A465

Milford
Haven

A40

A477

CWM CLYDACH

Llanelli

M4

Neath

Swansea

Port
Talbot

M4

Bridgend

Cardiff

Conwy, Conwy

P

The Conwy reserve was created by the RSPB following the construction of the Conwy tunnel. Shallow pools next to the estuary provide ideal feeding and roosting places for ducks, geese and some wading birds. From the visitor centre, where you can buy light refreshments and souvenirs, there is an excellent view of one of the pools, letting you get really close to the birds. There is a nature trail from the centre leading you to hides with views over the estuary and of the magnificent Conwy Castle.

Thousands of trees are being planted around the reserve and landscaping is still taking place.

Opening times: reserve – open at all times; centre – daily 10 am to 5 pm (or dusk if earlier).

non-members – adult £1, child 50p, concession 50p.

Location: Access from the A55 expressway. Leave the A55 at the exit signed to Conwy and Deganwy: the reserve entrance is on the roundabout above the expressway.

Llandudno Junction (0.75 mile/1.2 km);

0.5 mile/0.8 km every 20 minutes.

☎ 01492 584091

i 01492 592248

Visitor centre

Nature trails (shortest 0.5 mile/0.8 km, longest 2 miles/3 km) – all trails are suitable for pushchairs and wheelchairs

Birdwatching hides 3 (2 wheelchair accessible).

Black-tailed godwit

G Deaney (RSPB Images)

Shelducks breed at Conwy Nature Reserve.

Conwy Nature Reserve

C-D

P Cwm Clydach, Swansea

This mixed broadleaved woodland is home to breeding pied flycatchers, redstarts and buzzards. The Lower Clydach river flows through the centre of the reserve.
Opening times: public paths and trails open at all times.
Location: at Craig Cefn Parc, 2 miles north of Clydach at the New Inn public house on the B4291.
≈ Swansea;
🚌 Swansea to Craig Cefn Parc stop at reserve entrance, service hourly.
☎ 01792 842927
i 01792 468321
Nature trails 2 (shortest 1 mile/2 km, longest 7 miles/11 km). The shortest trail is suitable for wheelchairs and pushchairs.

P Dinas and Gwenffrwd, Carmarthenshire
S

This delightful reserve is set in the heart of mid-Wales. A boardwalk takes you through oakwood and then the trail continues to the fast-flowing river. Special viewing facilities have been set up at the reserve to watch red kites. Some parts of the nature trail are rugged and steep.
Opening times: reserve – open at all times; visitor centre – weekends and Bank Holiday weeks from Good Friday to 31 August.
🏵 non-members – £1 parking fee.
Location: 10 miles/16 km north of Llandovery on the minor road to Llyn Brianne.
≈ Llandovery (10 miles/16 km).
☎ 01550 760276 (during centre opening hours)
i 01550 720693
Visitor centre
Nature trails (2 miles/3 km), includes some rocky areas unsuitable for pushchairs and wheelchairs.

Dyffryn Wood, Powys

This reserve combines woodland and heather uplands. Red kites and pied flycatchers are just some of the birds that can be seen here. While the facilities are limited at the reserve, for those looking for a taste of the Welsh uplands, this is the place to visit.
Opening times: open at all times.
Location: 0.75 mile/1.2 km south of Rhayader on A470.
≈ Llandrindod Wells (12 miles/19 km);
🚌 from Rhayader stop at Llandrindod Wells, Wednesdays, Fridays and Saturdays only.
☎ 01597 811169
i 01597 810591
Nature trail (1 mile/1.6 km).

Kite country

Mid-Wales is the home of the red kite. Tourist centres in the area have joined to celebrate this beautiful bird of prey with displays and information. During the breeding season, live pictures are transmitted from nearby nests. There are kite centres at Llandovery, Llandrindod Wells, Llanwrtyd Wells and Nant y Arian Forest Centre near Ponterwyd and kites are fed in winter at Gigrin Farm in Rhayader.

C H Gomersall (RSPB Images)

Red kite

C H Gomersall (RSPB Images)

L

Lake Vyrnwy

P Lake Vyrnwy, Powys

Heather moorland, woodland, meadows, rocky streams and a large reservoir attract a wide variety of wildlife to this reserve set at the southern end of the Berwyn mountains. Dippers and kingfishers nest by the lake and rocky streams, while ravens and buzzards can be found on the moorland. Lake Vyrnwy is popular with both birdwatchers and families alike as it offers a full range of facilities, including a shop, nature trails and birdwatching hides. Visitors can drive around the reservoir by car.

Opening times: reserve – open at all times; visitor centre – 1 April to 24 December, daily 10.30 am to 5.30 pm, 1 January to 31 March, weekends only 10.30 am to 5.30 pm.

Location: 10 miles / 16 km west of Llanfyllin via the B4393 to Llanwddyn.

and Welshpool (25 miles / 40 km).
☎ 01691 870278
i 01691 870346
Visitor centre
Nature trails (shortest 1.5 miles / 2.5 km, longest 3 miles / 5 km)
Birdwatching hides 4 (1 wheelchair accessible).

Dipper

P Mawddach Valley, Gwynedd
††

This reserve offers superb scenery and beautiful walks through oak woodland. In the spring pied flycatchers, wood warblers and redstarts can be seen and heard in the wood. Ravens and buzzards can be seen throughout the year. The nature reserve has two trails, one of which is accessible to wheelchair users.

M-R

Opening times: reserve – open at all times; information centre – daily during Easter week and from Whitsun to the first week of September, 11 am to 5 pm (between Easter week and Whitsun weekends only 12 noon to 4 pm).
Location: 2 miles/3 km west of Dolgellau on the A493 next to the toll bridge at Penmaenpool.
≈ Morfa Mawddach (4 miles/6.5 km);
🚌 buses run along the A493 from Fairbourne.
☎ 01341 422071
i 01341 422888
Information centre – converted signal box.
Nature trails (shortest 0.5 mile/0.8 km, longest 2.5 miles/4 km).

Buzzards can be seen throughout the year at Mawddach Valley.

M Hamblin (RSPB Images)

⚡ Point of Air – Dee Estuary, Flintshire

As this reserve overlooks the Dee Estuary, it is a great place to watch estuary birds. It is at its best in the winter when thousands of wading birds and wildfowl feed on the mudflats. When the tide rises, the birds are forced onto the saltmarshes, giving even closer views.
Opening times: open at all times.
Location: access from Talacre, which is signed off the A548, 2 miles/3 km east of Prestatyn.
≈ Prestatyn;
🚌 daily from Flint or Prestatyn.
☎ 01352 780527
i 01745 889092
Local services in village
Nature trail (0.5 mile/0.8 km)
Birdwatching hides 1

†† Ramsey Island, Pembrokeshire
🏠
☕
🛏
S
🔭
👪
⚡

This dramatic offshore island has 400 feet/120 m seabird cliffs and fine examples of coastal heathland. The seabird cliffs are occupied between April and July. Choughs and wheatears breed on the island. In the autumn, a colony of breeding grey seals can also be seen.
Opening times: daily Easter to 31 October (closed Tuesdays).
🏠 non-members – adult £3, child £1.50, concession £1.50. Boat fares extra.
Location: offshore from St Davids.
≈ and 🚌 from Haverfordwest to St Davids.
🚤 boats leave from St Justinians lifeboat station, 2 miles west of St Davids.
☎ 0836 535733 (mobile phone) or 01437 720065.
i 01437 720392
Information centre
Nature trail (longest 3.5 miles/5.5 km, shortest 2 miles/3 km).

P ♠♠ ᴬⱽ South Stack Cliffs, Anglesey

Over 4,000 pairs of seabirds breed on the cliffs at South Stack every year. Between April and July you can watch them from the Ellin's Tower centre. Live video pictures are relayed back to the centre of one of the nests on the cliff. During the breeding season you can see puffins, fulmars, guillemots and razorbills.

Opening times: reserve – open at all times; information centre – daily (Easter to September) 11 am to 5 pm.

Location: 2 miles/3 km south of Holyhead on minor roads signed from Holyhead and Trearddur Bay.

⇌ Holyhead;

🚌 daily from Holyhead to South Stack.

☎ 01407 764973

i 01407 762622

Information centre
Public footpaths

Guillemots are among the breeding seabirds at South Stack.

Over 4,000 pairs of seabirds breed on the cliffs at South Stack.

V-Y

P Valley Lakes, Anglesey

During a stroll around this small reserve, you will find reed-fringed lakes and small rocky outcrops. A variety of ducks and other waterfowl can be seen on the lakes.

Opening times: open at all times.
Location: 2 miles/3 km south of Caergeilliog.
≈ Valley (4 miles/6.5 km), Rhosneigr (7 miles/11 km);
🚌 Maes Awyr/RAF Valley daily from Bangor and Holyhead.
☎ 01407 764973
i 01407 762622
Nature trail (2 miles/3 km).

P Ynys-hir, Cardiganshire

Set on the south side of the Dyfi estuary, this reserve mixes the delights of a Welsh oak woodland with the saltmarshes of the estuary. Spring is a wonderful time to visit the woodland when it is full of bird song and spring flowers. There are special nestboxes in the wood to encourage pied flycatchers to breed. The estuary is at its best for birds in the autumn and winter when large numbers of ducks and geese feed on the saltmarshes.

Teal

Opening times: reserve – daily 9 am to 9 pm (or sunset when earlier); visitor centre – March to October, daily 9 am to 5 pm, November to February, weekends only 10 am to 4 pm.
🏠 non-members – adult £2.50, child 50p, concession £1.50, family ticket £5.
Location: The visitor centre is signposted from Eglwys-fach, 1 mile/1.6 km off A487.
≈ Machynlleth (6 miles/9.5 km);
🚌 Eglwys-fach (4 buses Monday to Saturday, no Sunday service).
☎ 01654 781265
i 01654 702401
Visitor centre
Nature trails (shortest 0.5 mile/0.8 km, longest 3 miles/5 km) of which 1 mile/1.6 km wheelchair accessible
Birdwatching hides 7

Pied flycatcher

Merlin

Ynys-hir

C H Gomersall (RSPB Images)

Index